THE CAREGIVERS LEGAL SURVIVAL GUIDE

Navigating Through
The Legal System

Carolyn A. Brent, MBA

Copyright © 2017 by Carolyn A. Brent, MBA

All rights reserved. No parts of this book may be reproduced by any mechanical, photographic, or electronic process, or in the form of a phonographic, or electronic recording; nor may it be stored in a retrieval system, transmitted, or otherwise be copied for public or private use – other than for "fair use" as brief quotations embodied in articles and reviews without prior written permission of the publisher.

The information you are reading is directly taken from the Audio Version of the **"Why Wait?** *International Telesummit. Some of the words may not appear as Exact Translation of The English Audio Version*

Preparing LEGALLY "Why Wait? International Telesummit"

DAY 3: Preparing **LEGALLY**
DATE: Thursday November 10th, 2011
TIME: 12noon PST, 3pm EST, 8pm UK, 9pm Europe
LENGTH: 90 minutes

Hosted by

Lynn Serafinn, MAED, CPCC Author, coach, book promotions, Radio Host *"Turning up the volume of the music in your heart!"*

Co-Host

Carolyn A. Brent, is an American author, bodybuilder and elder-care legislation advocate She is best known as an award-winning advocate and the author of the best-selling books, *The Caregiver's Companion: Caring for Your Loved One Medically, Financially and Emotionally While Caring for Yourself* and *Why Wait? The Baby-Boomers Guide to Preparing Emotionally, Financially and Legally for a Parent's Death*, Brent is also the founder of the nonprofit organizations, Caregiver Story | Across All Ages | Grandpa's Dream.

VIP Guests

Ameenah Fuller, MPP - Business consultant, award-winning publisher, Founder of National Women's Professional Caucus (NWPC)

Carolyn Rosenblatt, RN, BSN - Author, attorney, mediator, public speaker, co-founder of AgingParents.com

TRANSCRIPTION DETAILS:

Date: 26-Oct-2015

Transcription results:

S1 00:07 Good evening, good morning, and good afternoon everyone and welcome to the Why Wait? Telesummit. My same is Lynn Serafinn. I'm a coach and author, and a promotional manager for Mind, Body, Spirit Authors and Self-Help Authors. I am your host throughout this three day event. Today is day three of three of our three day telesummit on where we will be exploring the topic of preparing emotionally, financially, and legally for the death of a parent as well as the bigger issue of aging and caregiving in general. I would like to bring your attention once again. I think most of you know by now that this special event is a gift to you sponsored by Carolyn A.

Brent who is the author of the brand new book called "Why Wait? The Baby Boomers Guide to Preparing Emotionally, Financially, and Legally for Parent's Death" which is having its official Amazon launch this coming Tuesday, November 15th, 2011. That's less than a week away. So later in the broadcast, we'll be telling you a bit about the book, and also how you can receive complete library of really excellent gift that are offered by many of Carolyn's friends and colleagues when you buy the book on the day of the launch next week.

S1 01:15 So for right now, I would like to introduce our mistress of ceremonies and my co-host this three day event Carolyn A. Brent. Carolyn A. Brent, MBA, she is a former clinical education manager in the - excuse me, I keep stumbling over that word - in the pharmaceutical industry and author of the book "Why Wait? The Baby Boomers Guide to Prepare Emotionally, Financially and Legally for a Parent's Death". She is - and I can vouch for this - she is an avid activist and an advocate working with the various members of the US Congress. One of those we're going to meet to somebody today who's running for Congress and will be talking about this for the purpose of creating change to protect seniors and also veterans from financial and medical abuse. And I must say also to work towards rights for caregivers as well. As you have heard especially on yesterday's broadcast we talked quite a lot about that. It's really quite a very passionate subject for Carolyn. She's appeared on many, many local, and national television and radio shows and is a much sought after keynote speaker. Good afternoon, Carolyn. How are you today?

S2 02:24 Good afternoon Lynn. It's a pleasure and an honor to be here on this very last day of the event. And I'm so grateful to have Carolyn Rosenblatt and also Ameenah Fuller on this conference day with me, I'm very happy, so thank you Lynn.

S1 02:39 Well, I'm delighted too and I can't wait to hear what they have to say because we have gotten so many questions on this topic that we're going to be covering today. I'll tell everybody about the topic in a minute. Let me introduce our two guests first so that you all get to know who we are going to be speaking with. First guest is Ameenah Fuller, MPP. She is an experienced business consultant and publisher of Looking In Politics Magazine or I should say Looking In Politics Magazine. Ameenah Fuller holds a Master's Degree in public policy and is a candidate for the California State Senate, District 25. She's a businesswoman for over 25 years. I tell you that's enough to want a holiday, isn't it Ameenah? And a CEO of a business consulting firm. She's an award-winning publisher of Looking In Publications and also the founder of the National Women's Professional Caucus Inland Empire established to promote professional women to reach their height of

S3 03:34 Thank you, Lynn. I am wonderful and I'm so happy to be on the call with the two Carolyns that are most important to this issue.

S1 03:43 And we're very glad that you're here as well. So let me introduce the second guest, and the second guest as we said is another Carolyn. It's Carolyn Rosenblatt, R.N., B.S.N. Carolyn Rosenblatt, and I'm going to have to say their names so when I'm directing questions I have to remember we have two Carolyns. Carolyn Rosenblatt is an author, an attorney, a mediator and a public speaker with over 40 years of experience in her combined professions of nursing and legal practice. She has worked extensively with geriatrics and legal issues of aging. And she is the co-founder of agingparents.com as well as the senior resource forum in educational non-profit. She's the author of a book called "The Boomer's Guide to Aging Parents", a help for those who are taking on the caregiver role in their lives. Welcome Carolyn Rosenblatt.

S4 04:34 Thank you so much.

S1 04:38 I'd like to know just in general - I asked this yesterday and I forgot to ask Ameenah before I introduced you Carolyn - what intention - and I'll ask Ameenah first and then Carolyn - what intention would you like to set today as we start this discussion? What would you like people to go away with by the end of this session? Just in a sentence, Ameenah.

S3 04:57 Well I would like people to learn how to communicate better about the issue of power of attorney, and the use and responsibility and duties of power of attorney.

S1 05:11 Great, great. And Carolyn, what would you like for people to take away at the end of today's broadcast?

S4 05:15 I would like people to have hope that they will be able to handle these complex issues that they have to face regarding their aging loved ones, and that even though it looks overwhelming, it really can be done if you know what you're doing.

S1 05:29 Fabulous. Carolyn B, you want to add anything to that before we start?

S2 05:33 Yes, I would like to just say I want a person to get off the call and not be a procrastinator, and go and take care of your paperwork immediately because tomorrow is not promised but we have today that we could count on. So that's what my hope is.

S1 05:53 Great. So we have communication, we have hope, and we have action. So that's fantastic. Let's hold that intention for this call. So listeners, today we'll be talking about preparing legally for parent stuff. This is a big topic and I think it's probably the one seeing that we've gotten the most questions from. And if you are listening live and you want to send in more questions, do send them to me because we'll be sending as many questions as we can in about an hour's time maybe a little bit less than an hours time. All you have to do if you're listening via webcast is to put the question in the box, you don't have to wait for me to say we're going to take questions. Just go ahead and write it and I'll get the questions later. and if you're listening on the phone later in the broadcast I'll tell you how raise your hand and ask your question. But for right now let's get into the discussion. The first half of the discussion is going to be more on kind of the theoretical understanding of the issue--

S2 06:53 Hello?

S3 06:54 Hello.

S1 06:55 Yes, it seemed to go blank for a second didn't it? Can you hear me now? [crosstalk] Some of these we touched on yesterday but I believe that it will warrant going over just a little bit again, and it is on the topic of legal rights for caregivers, because that's an issue, and I know Carolyn Brent yesterday was very passionate about it. Ameenah, what would you like to say about-- what's the situation for legal rights for caregivers, and I understand were talking about only the United States because some of the people on the call are not calling from the United States?

S3 07:30 Well, I want to say first of all that Carolyn and I, we co-authored an article on the scary side of the power of attorney, and that was for Looking In Politics. And with that article is one of the concerns and issues that I was looking to address because it actually happened with my own family where power of attorney became an abusive situation. Power of attorney in itself is just the legal document to take control of maybe your parent or grandparent's financial, medical issues that may arise once they have become a little bit more demented in the process of aging. And so that's what happened, initially, with my grandmother. She became a little bit more demented over time and as she reached the age of 96, there was an issue with the power of attorney that was first drafted by my mom with a will, and then the power of attorney and the trust. And then there was fighting that ensued with the siblings that caused a problem with the power of attorney being that it was undermined by another sibling with another power of attorney. So that power of attorney superseded the other power of attorney.

S3 09:00 However, the caregiver which happened to be my mom was the caregiver for my grandmother for 25 years. And she had been providing all these services as a caregiver, and she had been doing excellent job. She had recommendation letters from all the folks that my grandmother had experienced to her life. And my mother was doing a fantastic job for her. The sibling rivalry and the undercurrents of financial gain causes this problem as a person starts to lose their mental capacity. So then you have someone challenging the power of attorney, and that's basically what happened in this case where my auntie under my mother's power of attorney, and had my grandmother sign another power of attorney when she was incapable of making that decision. So then, that power of attorney superseded my mom's power of attorney. This is what caused me to wonder how this could happen. How someone could come in and undermine a 25-year caregiver without any kind of real validation. Also, abuse of Adult Protective Services, filing false claims against my mother in reference to my grandmother's care. So, all of this pointed to the direction of how can we prevent power of attorney abuse. And also the abuse of adult protective services with false claims from siblings for financial gain for a senior, to take control of a senior, and to actually abuse that senior financially and emotionally. How do we prevent this?

S3 10:54   So, I did my research and luckily God put both Carolyn and I together to work on this article. And I think we brought out some of the aspects that I want to see transfer into legislation which is going to hopefully safeguard seniors rights. And some of those things, I call it the six points of safeguarding a seniors right. One, I think what we need to do, and this is in the United States legislation, is that we need to look at screening the background of some of these potential POA's. And I'm talking about the individuals seeking POA's, there needs to be some type of screening process in placed. We also need to look individuals as far as their physical and mental capabilities and they take control of a seniors life because some people are not capable of handling this responsibility. We also need to look at the time that they they've invested in the care of the senior. Have they invested any time or did they just come last week and decide that they want to take over my mom or my dad and be in control because I want their finances to be over? What is their reason for wanting to come and become a caregiver? How much time have they invested? I think that should be part of the legislation. We need to fine tune how attorneys and other agencies work to together to identify some of these triggers that are going on, that are causing such a gap between abuse of power of attorney and the good that power of attorney can really do if it's executed and used properly. And--

S1 12:53 Let me interject just for a minute, Ameenah, because we have an attorney on the panel and I'm sure listening to this horror story, actually, that you're telling, which it is quite horrible of this story of what happened in your family. Carolyn Rosenblatt, as you're listening this, as an attorney, what are your reflections on this?

S4 13:12   I am very sorry that that happened to Ameenah, and I'm also sorry to say that in my work as a consultant and a mediator for families, this is not unusual. I get questions about this on a regular basis. The great thing about a power of attorney is that when it is done properly and when it is used well, it can save the entire family from having to go to court and have a conservatorship or guardianship placed over that elder. In the wrong hands, it is a license to steal. The difficulty that we have with power of attorney is that it was meant to be something that people could use without the court having to get involved, because the court is typically much more involved in the process of a guardianship or conservatorship. You have to go to court to get that because a court order is required to put that into place, evidence has to be presented. No such place card exists for a power of attorney. So we have a real conflict in the intention of this kind of document which is used all over the country very often, and the concept of a conservatorship which is an expensive proposition and a very burdensome proposition. So we would indeed have to create another bureaucracy somewhere within our government to screen the potential powers of attorney the biggest problem--

S1 14:39   Carolyn, can you explain what a conservatorship is? I'm sorry, Carolyn, can you explain what a conservatorship because I think most people who are in this situation probably know what a power of attorney is, so what do you mean by a conservatorship

S4 14:51 Well, in some states, California in particular is called conservatorship. In most other places its called guardianship. A guardianship in legal means by which the court based upon evidence places someone in charge of either a person's whole personal life, it's called guardianship of the person, or of their estate which means all of their money and property, or both. And that usually comes into play when a person is losing their capacity as with dementia or Alzheimer's disease, something like that. So it's a formal proceeding that requires reporting and monitoring by the judge, and the courts are a little reluctant to grant these most places because of the difficulty of taking away someone's rights. We do have the right to life and liberty and so forth, and we want to protect that right, we want to allow people that right, unless there's a very good reason to take it away. And the courts require a significantly high standard to prove that someone should have that taken away. It's not as high as beyond a reasonable doubt like in a criminal court, but it's much more than just more likely than not that they need it. So that's what a conservatorship is. It's a formal court order lawyers typically require, you have to go back to court, you have to do accountings, you have to show where every penny is spent. It's quite a big deal.

S4 16:15 And it also removes the person's ability to do everything independently. They can't decide where they're going to live. They can't decide what they're going to do with their lives anymore. They have some rights but they're very limited. And the monitoring of these conservatorships or guardianships varies considerably from state to state. There is abuse and neglect, as you can imagine, within this sort of framework of having a person formally take over your life. But within a power of attorney, it's a very different thing because there isn't any court monitoring. There's no one to even vet the person who would be the power of attorney. And as happened with Ameenah and happens in lots of places, some unscruplous person, relative or not, comes in after the elder is vulnerable, usually while they are still possessed with some abilities and persuade them often without difficulty to sign a power of attorney. And the other power of attorney on this is revoked or is no good anymore.

S4 17:17 So that gives the ruthless person, shall we say, all the rights that someone who would be their conservator have. They can do just about everything. There is a form for this. They can take over the person's life and the money and everything else. So it's a real dilemma that we have in our society because so many people have dementia, 5.2 million people in the United States along not counting all the people in other country, and that's the ones who are diagnosed. Not all of them in millions more who have symptoms, or developing these problems for years and have not been formally diagnosed. It is a huge growing problem. I think Ameenah is exactly right that we need to change the law, and that we need to have some process however basic for screening people who are going to take over such an enormous responsibility over the life of another especially when they sashay in at the last minute, when the person is already demented, and try to behave as if that person has the capacity to find such a document. In Ameenah's case that could have been something but it would have takes court's action to validate that second power of attorney.

S1 18:28   It's shocking, actually, as I'm listening to this. One, you're both-- when you're both giving these accounts, you realize that there is a tremendous - what's the word - opportunity, I suppose, for abuse of not just the caregivers, but also the elderly. Carolyn Brent as you're listening to all of this I'm sure you're there with loads of things you want to elaborate on what you've just heard.

S2 18:55   Well, the key thing-- I've spoken with Carolyn Rosenblatt very, very intently, and also Ameenah Fuller, and they're right on the money with the subject matter because it's real people are turning their backs on the medical profession, attorneys are turning their back, even judges, in my particular case, my family member went through three jurisdictions filing abuse charges, financial and medical abuse charges against me, and as soon as we got before the judge, she'd say "Oh, Your Honor. I drop the charges." So that's one case and then as soon as I walk out of the courthouse, I would be given another restriction that I couldn't see my dad. It was abuse charges. In another county, my sibling did this in three different counties, and the very last county I'd gone to, I told the judge, I said "Your Honor. Please, my sister is dragging me through three jurisdictions, taking me before the court and dropping the charges as soon as I have my attorney, I have witnesses, I have my father's doctor, which, when you pay a doctor to close down their practice, to go to court and sit with you, trust me, it's not cheap. It's up in the thousands of dollars because they don't want to spend their whole entire day when they're practicing medicine sitting in a court.

S2 20:26 So, Dr. [Fidel?] actually went with me three different times. He never got a chance to speak with the judge because my sibling would drop the charges. So what inevitably happened, that very last judge said if I wanted to press charges against my sibling, I would have to take her yet to another court and sue for defamation of character. So, the system, they know that this is happening, but the courts are safeguarded where they cannot perceive another something that's been dropped. It's like it doesn't exist. However, it's on my record that I was dragged to court three times which absolutely infuriates me so that's why I wrote the book, that's why I draw my research, I discovered Carolyn Rosenblatt and I actually drove over to her practice to meet her and her husband. After speaking with her I felt like, okay, I'm not the only one that this is happening to, but I wish I would have met Carolyn Rosenblatt ten years ago or even five years ago, because she has the knowledge that I wish I would have known when I was caring for my dad for 12 years from the families that-- Carolyn, you're doing a great job, that a girl, do a great job. I wish I would have known about a sibling contract. I didn't know that until-- like I said I was doing research and I stumbled upon Carolyn. I said, "I've got to meet you, please let me come and meet you." And the rest is history.

S1 22:03 Let's go onto that topic and there's so many ways we can go here because there's just so many other issues here. I mean, I don't understand why you can't get an order protection against somebody for harassment and in a case like that, I actually don't understand. The effect doesn't sound-- it sounds like not harassment to me from my simple minded mind about legal things, so it sounds like-- but let's talk about sibling contract law and also because I know Carolyn Brant had said this to me and she said it on the call yesterday. There's a big difference in US federal laws and state laws and obviously county and things like that. The fact that somebody can be tried in a county after a county, after county, that's amazing to me. So, let's talk about sibling contract law and also perhaps how it might differ or any of these kinds of laws might differ from federal state and local areas. Ameenah, how about you, why don'y you share with us what you know on that subject?

S3 23:09 Well, I was researching this very issue because the issue that we had was with Adult Protective Services and the false claims that were made. This is also an issue and I think that had affected Carolyn as well. In Texas law, they prohibit false claims of elder abuse. But this happened in Oklahoma with my family, and they don't have those things in place. So like you were saying, each state is different, so each state has different laws as it relates to Adult Protective Services and the false claims that are made by whatever party, whether that's a sibling or not. And also, I just read recently that Florida enacted a law which is called 709FS. It is a power of attorney law under that chapter, 709FS, and what it does is it defines some of the gray areas of power of attorney. And what this new Florida Law - which came out in October of 2011, that was just last month - is talking about the duties and how someone should act in good faith with a power of attorney, which I think is important. It also talks about the duties of acting lawly and for the sole benefit of the principal, and it talks about the duties to act with care and competence and diligence. And some of these things need to be spelled out, and I don't think these things have been spelled out in the past. So each state is doing something different. In California, I want to propose some of these types of protection for power of attorney on a state level, but we also need to advocate for this on a federal level as well, I think.

S1 25:10 I think you really opening up another door to great exploitation if it isn't done on a federal level. I think you're absolutely right. Carolyn Rosenblatt, Carolyn Brent mentioned sibling contract law. What can you tell us about that?

S4 25:25 Well, there isn't exactly sibling contract law, there's contract law. And I think that lawyers who are familiar with aging issues and caregiver issues are more likely to be creative in applying basic contract law to situations where we have siblings who may be sharing a caregiver role. But it's not something you can look up in a book and pull out and give somebody a form, although people have asked me for one. I said, "Look, every elders needs are different, every caregivers needs are going to be unique, so we don't have a special form you can get." However, the essential principles of contract law can apply to any situation like this where you are giving up something, doing something maybe to your own detriment, like quitting your job or contributing your labor, or going to live with your parent, or taking in your aging relative, and there can be something exchanged for that. And, if there's a lot of labor involved, as there will inevitably be with anyone who has dementia, Alzheimer's disease in particular, you can have trade off. For example, if one sibling is going to be the primary caregiver, and to live with the elder or give that person daily care, perhaps they're going to inherit more at the end, or perhaps if the elder has the means, they're going to get paid for doing it. And, yes, if the purpose was reasonable and legitimate to get paid for providing care for your relative, including your parent, or your grandparent, or your aunt, or whoever it may be. But, these things are not generally thought of ahead of time, they're not thought out. People don't take the time or trouble to say, "You know, this looks like it's going to be a long haul. Mom's just been diagnosed with Alzheimer's disease, we need to think this through and get somebody to help us drop an agreement that's going to make us feel more fair.

S1 27:17 I had a friend in New York who her mother had a pretty severe case of Alzheimer's which meant that they had - she and her husband, and her two young sons - had to move back into the mother's house which was actually the - we're here Carolyn, can you hear us? - which was actually the childhood home. And she nursed the mother until the mother actually passed away and the house was left to her. The sister freaked out totally, felt totally left out in all of this stuff, but the fact is the sister didn't do anything. This woman had moved her entire family into this house to be a 24-hour caregiver for a woman who was completely incontinent and would go out in the streets and start shouting and things like that. But her sister had an absolute fit over it. So how can that be avoided? Carolyn Brent, I know you're not a lawyer but I'm going to ask you anyway because you've done so much research on this, how can that be avoided - that kind of arguing about that after the fact? She just came back. Dear, so you didn't even hear my question?

S2 28:30   Sorry, my phone dropped.

S1 28:32   You seemed to be on the line twice, so I thought you were there. I'm sorry. I'm seeing you twice on the switchboard. Well, let me address that to Carolyn Rosenblatt and then Carolyn Brent, you can come back in. How can that be avoided, Carolyn Rosenblatt?

S4 28:44   I think first of all the sibling who agrees to move in and take care of mom, knowing that she has advanced Alzheimer's disease, bring her entire family there, should not do so blindly. That's a lot of work. It's going to take a lot of time. Alzheimer's disease and all other dementias do not remain stable over time. They are progressive deteriorating illnesses, they get worst. It's more work over time, not less, and to walk into it blindly with no idea of what the consideration that is if something of value should be in exchange for what you're doing is just plain not thinking ahead. So in order to prevent that kind of blow up that how it happens and these are not uncommon scenarios either, you need this to think it through and say to your sibling, "Look, I'm going to give up everything. And I'm going to be taking care of mom. If you want to share the load, let's talk about what would be fair. If you don't want to share the load, let's talk about what would be fair to me and by families because this going to affect all of us." And once that agreement is made assuming it can be. "Let's get this put down in writing and both sign off on it so we don't forget what happened." I'm a strong believer in using the power of the written word. As a lawyer, that's what I'm trained to understand. It's a good way to do things that are agreements. Put them in writing. Make sure that's legally sufficient. It wouldn't be that big of a deal for a confident elder law or elder care attorney to draw up such an agreement and help you work that out so that it doesn't hit the fan after mom or dad passes.

S1 30:13 I think there's great power in just having another person there who's mediating. I mean you called yourself a mediator before, and to just get somebody there so it's not siblings, just bringing up all their old history with each other, which I think is what happened with Carolyn Brent a little bit. Carolyn Brent, as you are listening to us talking about sibling- there is no such thing as sibling contract law- but there is such thing as a sibling contract. If you could have done it all over again, when would you have sat down with your sister or other siblings, when would you have sorted it out and what would you have done? If you could turn back the clock and do it again.

S2 31:04 That is an excellent question for me because I tried for many, many, many years to sit down with my family. I went as far as putting together a five-inch binder with all of my father's medical history from all the doctors, all of my father's financial history, everything that I knew of, and then I also put in my financial history. My family wouldn't even look at the book. It's huge. And I even had taken it to court to show the judge, and the judge said, "Put that book down or I'm going to get you for attempted court." Because I wanted try to prove I had been trying to have that conversation with my family. Now what I would have done differently - once again, it took me to go through research - I would not have gone as blindly in those early days, back in 1997 when the family was going, "That a girl, you're doing a great job. You're doing a great job." I would have then gotten a third party involved, like a Carolyn Rosenblatt, and I would have said "What can I do in my family to safeguard myself for just in case on the back end if they pull shenanigans?

S2 32:14 I never thought my family would have done this. That's why I was so devastated and shocked and torn and angry at what has happened. So not only have I been torn away from my father, which I will have to live with for the rest of my life, I was torn away from my job as a clinical education manager that I had worked towards for many, many years. I had to step away from that job and go back to being a sale representative, which was like an entry level position because I could no longer travel anymore. Because I had to take care of dad. So just knowing that I had given so much up. I went from age I think 47 to 54 overnight. I don't remember my 40s, my mid-40s at all. Excuse me, I went from 39, the age 39 to like 54, that everything, all my 40s literally disappeared because I used all of that time and spent that time caring for dad only to get literally blocked in the back that this is the key thing. I grew up in a separate home from my brothers and sisters. So everything that I experienced, it more than likely went back to childhood where the resentment started, because I grew up with dad. I was like an only child that lived with dad because I ran away from an abusive mother. So it started making me realized, where did all this started? It started way back then when I was 12 years old.

S1 33:51   Really good point, Carolyn, because I know--

S2 33:53   If I had to do it all over again, that's what I would have done.

S1 33:57   And I think it's very important for us to realize that--

S2 33:59   Hello?

S1 34:00   --when our parents die--

S2 34:01   Oh, my God.

S1 34:03   Carolyn? Can you not hear me anymore?

S2 34:05   Hello?

S1 34:06   Yes, we can hear you, Carolyn [laughter]. I don't know what phone. She seems to be keeping on losing connection. But anyway, she'll call back. And what I was going to say is I think that it's a well-learned point that when our parents die, all the old family has to restart to a comeback. I think because Carolyn's phone got knocked off the line, I think it's a good time for me to take the break to talk about Carolyn's book, and then after the break we'll come to talking about more practical side of this discussion. We've been talking now kind of about the situation, what is the situation. The fact is that families argue, that they don't know how to communicate, the fact that there is a lot of room for exploitation in the legal system. So we are going to hold that, and then in the second half of the conversation, we're going to be talking about a checklist of necessary documents that you need. How do you approach a lawyer, things that you need to be sure are in your documentation so that so they are set up right. And just basically how you can actually protect yourself from litigation as had happened with Carolyn which was really tragic. And also in Ameenah's case. So, we'll get to that in a few minutes. But before we do that, I just want to take a couple of minutes to remind you that this whole three-day event is sponsored by Carolyn Brant who I think finally got back on the phone. You're there, right Carolyn?

S2 35:33 I don't know why phone keeps dropping, sorry.

S1 35:36 Okay. We heard you but you don't hear us. We heard you say, "Oh my God." and then you disappeared [laughter]. So anyways, Carolyn Brant, is the person who is sponsoring this event in celebration for the launch of her book which is called "Why Wait? The Baby Boomers' Guide to Preparing Emotionally, Financially and Legally for a Parent's Death." It's coming out on Tuesday, this coming Tuesday, November 15th, 2011. I've mentioned this to you before, if you're listening via webcast and you're looking on the screen, you'll see a big button there that says "Click here for free gift on November 15th." something like that. And if you click on that button you'll see a page that lists the gifts that people are offering. It's very simple. You buy the book, you get the gift. It's very simple. I'm giving away some audio on overcoming-- not overcoming but a spiritual journey of depression and things like that, which I've been told that they've been very inspirational. I know Ameenah's giving away a video and also an article on the scary side of power of attorney. And Carolyn Rosenblatt, I've forgotten what gifts you're giving. Do you remember what you're giving?

S2 36:51   It's a webcast that we've done and it's really about communication and family.

S1 36:56   Great. And so all of the gifts that are going to be coming are really a great enhancement for the book. They're all things that you can use to kind of get you in that right place to utilize this book. Again, the book is coming out on Tuesday. You will receive - I just want to let you know - you will receive a reminder on Monday night probably around just after midnight Pacific Time going into Tuesday, that the book is now available. It's in paperback and in Kindle. If you buy the book either in paperback or in Kindle on that day, you can get all the gifts. It's as simple as that. And it's really just to thank you, and it's a way of us supporting Carolyn in this important work. I've been working with Carolyn now it's close to a year. As you can hear in her voice, she's one of the most passionate people I've ever met on a particular subject. She's as sincere as can be about this, and I know that when you get the book you'll find it to be a very practical guide to going through these very emotional and overwhelming issues. So check it out. Again, it's called Why Wait? coming on Tuesday. And if you are not looking at the link right now - if you're on the phone in other words - if you go to babyboomersguide.org and then click on the link - I think it says something like book launch or something like that, I'm not quite sure what button we have - but it will also take you to the page with the bonus gifts. But never fear, I will send you a reminder and you will be taken right to the page where you can get all of those gifts on Tuesday. So, thanks for that. Carolyn, did you want to add anything before we go on to the second half of the conversation?

S2 38:34 Actually, no, you did a great job. I'm just excited that it's almost over, yay [laughter].

S1 38:41 We've worked so hard. I met Carolyn when she was still writing the book and we've gone through the whole thing with the cover, and the editing, and the publishing, and the blah, blah blah. It's a big deal to put a book together, great. So, thank you Caroline. As we said, this time we're going to be approaching practical things, and then after 20 minutes or so, we're going to start taking questions from the audience. I already have a lot of them that have come in in advance. If you've just tuned in, please do. If you're on the webcast, please do start writing your questions in the Q&A box on the screen because I'll be taking them in about 20 minutes. If you're on the phone or Skype, I will tell you how you can raise your hand and ask questions later. It would be around the top of the hour. Before I want to do this, wait. I must do this because I always forget. Before we get into the conversation, Carolyn and Ameenah, can you please tell everybody your websites? I'm going to send it to them in an email, but can you also just tell everyone your websites now? Maybe Ameenah first?

S3 39:43 My website - I have two - one is lookinginpolitics.webs.com, the other one is ameenahfullerforcaliforniastatesenate.webs.com.

S1 39:59 And Carolyn Rosenblatt?

S4 40:01 Agingparents.com.

S1 40:04 That's easy enough, aging parents.

S4 40:07 Agingparents.com.

S1 40:08 Agingparents.com. Carolyn Brent, you might as well say your sites, too, because most people have found them already, but you might as well say them.

S2 40:16 I have two. I have caregiverstory.com and I have babyboomersguide.org

S1 40:25 Right. And as I said, I'm going to send this to everybody. My main site is spiritauthors.com. That's where I work with authors. I've got others for my books and stuff, but that's the main one for tonight. Spiritauthors.com. On to the discussion. Let's get to the practical side. Let's start making a checklist of legal documentation that people need. And so that we don't have one person giving all of it, let's play Round Robin. Everybody say one legal document you must have. Ameenah, I bet I know which one you're going to say.

S3 40:58   Well, I'm going to say the living will.

S1 41:01   Living will? Carolyn Rosenblatt?

S4 41:06   I think people need wills and trusts even if they don't have a lot of money. Having wills and trusts is crucial because part of the process of putting those together means they will also likely have both the health care directive, which Ameenah's calling a living will, and the durable power of attorney.

S1 41:23   So a living is the same as a healthcare directive?

S4 41:26   Yes.

S1 41:28   Because some people may not understand that, so that's great. So we have--

S4 41:30   Correct. A lot of different names. It's also called the power of attorney for healthcare.

S1 41:35   It's also called the power of attorney for healthcare. That's what makes things so confusing to people. The power of attorney for healthcare, healthcare directives, and living will - those are all the same things and wills and trusts - Carolyn B., what else can people have? What are the other checklists to the central document people [inaudible]

S2 41:53 They need to have a medical directive just in case something happens and everyone needs a medical directive. What are your wishes? And also I dual on which she just said, dual power of attorney.

S4 42:08 They're all the same.

S1 42:09 A healthcare directive, a durable power of attorney for healthcare, a living will, those are all the same thing.

S2 42:15 Yes.

S1 42:16 It's a document that enables you when you are incompetent to have someone take over as your agent and carry out your wishes. So specifying what you want is part of creating that document. And it's a form. It's available everywhere, it's free, you can get it from your doctors office, you can get it from your clinic, you can get it on the internet. The laws vary from state to state about certain specifics, but generally speaking if you have one, it's good anywhere.

S2 42:47 I want to add something, Lynn.

S1 42:49 Yes, please.

S2 42:51 Advance directives. And with my grandmother's case, there was a portion of the living will that specified hospice, but it did not specify the actual type of hospice that she wanted. I know for a fact that she would only have wanted hospice in terminal illness, and she wanted to have hospice care at home. But because it wasn't really spelled out in the living will, my aunt decided to put her in hospice with comfort care which means that you don't get any food or nutrition, you're basically given pain medication and allowed to die even though she did not have a terminal illness. This can be very tricky because the hospice was not really spelled out the type of hospice care that she wanted to have in the living will. But we knew, based on what she had indicated, what she wanted. But my aunt did not fulfill those wishes as she had requested verbally, but she went with the living will. So the living will, I think, and those advanced directives, they need to really be specific as to what they really want in terms of that. But my grandmother did not know the differences between hospice care, and comfort care, and all of those things. That's why it's important with Carolyn's book, Why Wait? is to get these things in order way in advance so you can spell it out before you enter a period of dementia where you don't understand these aspects of these documents.

S1 44:42 As we're talking about this, since this is aimed at baby boomers - I mean I'm almost 57, my mother died at 69. That's a wake up call. And it does say to us, we owe it to our children. At our age, baby boomers, we owe it to our children not to make things complicated for them. So while we're still vital, it's really worth it to make the lives of our children very easy and make things very spelled out for them. So it's not just about preparing for a parent's death. I think it's also making life easier for our children and grandchildren as we age so that-- that's what I'm thinking when I'm with listening--

S4 45:21 Yes, it's a necessity. And Carolyn B. said it well. This you don't wait. This is something you do right now. If you walk away from this telesummit and there's one thing you do, one action you'll going to take, it's get your healthcare directive done. And go through every single page and spell out in detail what you want. If you are in a last illness and you don't want to get anything other than pain medication, put that down. If you want to get IVs, write that down. If you want to get food and water, put that down, assuming you're able to swallow. We have something else in California which I think will be spreading to other places, although it's fairly new, it's called Physician Ordered Life Sustaining Treatment, POLST. It's another form that's really more specific and detailed concerning what your last wishes will be. There's also something called Five Wishes, which can be purchased on the internet. And all of these things are ways of specifying with more clarity for whomever is in charge what it is you do and don't want if you cannot speak for yourself toward the end of your life. There are a lot of choices. So take the time, think it through, be specific, ask questions, get the information so that your healthcare directive is going to make it really easy for the people you love.

S1 46:42 Carolyn, do you have another document-- Carolyn B., do you have another document because I have a question that's really relevant to this discussion that I want to ask that somebody sent. Is there some other documents that we should be looking at that we haven't said yet?

S2 46:56 I think we're covering it all. Do you ladies agree with that?

S4 47:00 Yeah, that's the big three [crosstalk] [inaudible] health care directive, and all of the names is also called by as three - there's big three.

S1 47:11 And the sibling contract idea? What's that about?

S4 47:13 The idea of a contract is really not end of life planning, that's caregiving planning. And it kind of varies from everybody and everybody doesn't need one. Everybody doesn't have a sibling, or a sibling who's willing to pitch in and do anything. But I would say that if you are in a situation where you're elder is failing or they have shown you some memory loss issues, or you think that you or one of the other siblings is going to have to take care of that person, that's when you need to talk about a contract.

S2 47:40   Absolutely.

S3 47:42   I agree--

S2 47:44   I think that's key. I have a question to ask Carolyn R. Have you ever in your 40 years experience had families fight about who's going to change their loved ones adult diapers or who's going to take them to the grocery store. Do people fight about that ever?

S4 48:04   They certainly do. And in my role as a mediator, I am dealing with family conflict all the time. Some of them are simple and we can sit down and it doesn't require any courts or lawsuits or any of that. We just try to make agreements. They get written down by me. Everybody signs off and then they've got a contract among family members. People will fight about anything. I was settling a case in court one day helping the judges, because we do from time to time as volunteers, and these family members were fighting with their stepmother over a box of T-shirts. They had been in court for two years over this case and it was finally settled by agreeing the lady, their stepmother, who did not care about the box of T-shirts agreed to give it up and they said "Okay. We finally got something of dad back, now we can put this case to rest."

S4 48:56 Now, how did we get to that? I finally had to ask them, what do you really want? What do you really want in all this? You don't want to keep fighting, do you? No, we don't want to keep fighting. What is it that has meaning for you, that you hope to take away from this particular court action that you've engaged in for all this time? Well, we just want something of dad. Well, can you name something? Well, there's this T-shirt collection he had. And I'm thinking, for god's sake, why didn't they do this at the beginning? Well, they needed the help and they didn't have it and that's how it went. But yes, it's like divorces. People will fight over somebodies tea set for six years. It's just a symbol of something. It isn't the thing itself.

S2 49:31 I got it.

S4 49:32 They do fight over changing diapers. They do fight over who is going to take dad to appointments. They fight over everything. But it really sometimes calls up old sibling conflicts and resentments that go back to childhood as Carolyn B. mentioned and then this thing that they're fighting about becomes the vehicle for expressing that underlying distress. They can't be worked out, that's where the hope is. All of these things can be worked out. You just have to get the right help and be willing and know what to do.

S2 50:00 Very well said.

S3 50:02 I want to add to that too, Carolyn R. is that with the new law that's in Florida, they are looking at the co-agents part of that power of attorney to allow these co-agents again on power of attorney to act independently as well with decision making. And I think that is the part that could have helped my family with what we had or what we were going through because the power of attorney that my aunt created, there were co-agents on that power of attorney, but they could not act independently. And this new law that is going on in Florida which is one that I'm going to be looking at in terms of creating laws in California is it allows the co-agents to act independently even the children that are signed on to this power of attorney. They can act independent of the initiator of the power of attorney which would be that principal person. But they can act also independent on decision making. What do you think your thoughts are on that as it relates to some of the issues that have been going on with the abuse of power of attorney with the co-agents now that this law opens the door for that? What do you think in terms of those contracts with siblings and as far as power of attorney and the co-agent?

S4 51:45 I think that co-agents on a power of attorney can be a mistake and here's why. If you have two people, for example, who had equal authority on the power of attorney, and they can each act independently, the person who says no has all the power. Because when the other person can act, and if they're supposed to do this independently then the power of attorney really isn't any good. What I think makes more sense, and I always recommended there be one person appointed as the agent and power attorney, one person, same with the healthcare directive. You can ask advice if you want to, you can get other people's input, but somebody, one person needs to be in charge to avoid ugly fights outside mom or dad's hospital room in the corridor. That's a very unpleasant place to be working out your disagreements. Now, what do we do with these ideas, these problems that you've identified, Ameenah, where somebody comes in. And I think we need to be more creative in the initial drafting of the power of attorney itself. It's a form that you can get for free on the internet, or you can use everything that's in that form and put something at the bottom of it when your elder is still completely confident and has no dementia, no diminished capacity and say, "I agree that this power of attorney will not be changed unless." And you can put something in there about I have been deemed fully confident to do so by a psychologist through testing. Or you can say, "My physician, my treating doctor says that I'm confident." Whatever is you want to put in there to give some protection for this elder being taken advantage of because when people have dementia, they are sitting ducks.

S1 53:28 That's very relevant to question that - let's see - Dale in South Bend, Indiana asked. It says, "My mother's durable power of attorney dates back to 1989. The key information in it is still valid but I question the legality of it being that old. For instance, if she became incapacitated tomorrow, would her durable power of attorney still be valid? Or-- I can't read the rest of it because I scribbled this from something else. Would it still be valid regarding long term care?

S4 54:06 Would you like me to answer that question?

S1 54:08 If you feel inclined.

S4 54:11 The thing that makes the durable power of attorney durable is that it's good for life. And it says in a specific language by statue, that is by state law, that it is good regardless of incapacity. So if the person who was competent in 1989 articulated her wishes and said this is who I want in charge, and this is what they're going to be in charge of and I give them complete authority to do this and that, it's good for life.

S1 54:38 So that's the answer to that deal. And one other question that's relevant to what we're talking about now. Rory in Florida, has been asking lots of questions throughout the three days. She's asking, can these legal documents be drawn up by a late person and witnessed and notarized or do they have to have to have a lawyer and--

S4 54:59 I'll answer that specific second legal question. A durable power of attorney at least in my state, and I believe this is also true in other states does not require an attorney. It has sweeping legal consequences and its good to get legal advice about it. I recommend that you at least talk to someone about what it means if you are going to sign or if mom or dad is going to sign one. You talk to a lawyer about it because it really means somebody else can do just about anything to you, and for you, just about anything. So it doesn't require a lawyer but it's prudent to get legal advise. They always have to be notarized to prove that its your signature but you do not have to go to court and the law does not require that you have it drawn up by a lawyer. It's a standardized form. In California there are fillable forms that you can just get from the internet or produced for everyone's use

S1 55:55 I hear you say that and what I'm thinking is that I know so little about the possible things that could go wrong apart from this discussion that I would feel a lot safer if I had a lawyer who could say, "What about this or what about that?" and then I could make sure that it's spelled out correctly and I didn't just say, "Oh well, I'll just put this". And then it wasn't, as Ameenah was saying, it wasn't detailed enough. It didn't have the details.

S2 56:24 The standardized form has a list of things. It basically has language at the beginning that says,

"I'm competent and I'm going to make this person have authority. I'm appointing them as my agent, this is who they are, and they are allowed to do the following things", and it has a list. They can do banking, and real estate transactions, and handle money, and buy and sell real estate. It goes on and on. There's a blank at the bottom where a person can just initial it and it says all of the above. So you can limit it by saying no to any one of those things or you can leave it very comprehensive. But in any case one is not bound to use that form, you can take the language from that form and as I was suggesting earlier, add some provisions in it, although we don't have laws that say we need to do this now, we can still do it. We can still say "If I become incapacitated or if somebody in my family thinks I am and they want to change this, this is what is going to be required before I will sign anything else." So then it's there at a time when we know they're competent and we were requiring some other measure, getting tested by a psychologist, for example, to determine if they have dementia or indications of significant diminished capacity, that would be a really good thing to have there.

S1 57:43 So I want to let the audience if they want to ask live questions for you on the phone now. If you want to press-- if you have a question and please stick to asking question. We actually don't have time to listen to long scenarios. So really, think clearly what question you'd like to ask and if you want to ask a question press "star two" on your telephone keypad. That will raise your hand and I can see you on the switchboard and I will and I will unmute your line in the order of which questions. And there's a caller and it's somebody on Skype. So I don't know-- hold a second, there's somebody on Skype. Hello Skype caller, say hello and see if it's you.

S5 58:26   Hello?

S1 58:27   Hello. Yes, that's you.

S5 58:29   It is? I'm not on Skype, but--

S1 58:32   It says Skype. What's your name and what's your question please?

S5 58:36   Vanessa Thomas Jones and I'm an old, dear friend of Carolyn's from back in the day. If she's still on, Carolyn Brant.

S2 58:45   I'm on.

S1 58:46   Yes, she is.

S5 58:47   From Denver.

S2 58:48   Hi.

S1 58:48   It's her party, she has to be here [laughter].

S5 58:51 Carolyn, I just want to express my sorrow with all the things you've gone through. And I just wanted you to know I wish I had had this earlier, but I just finished completing my trust for my family. I was one of the fortunate ones where my mother planned everything for us. She didn't have a trust or a will, but we put everything in me and my sister Cathy's name, the house and everything before she passed, and after my father passed, so we didn't have that problem. Is there a problem with doing that type of transaction? I spent a lot of money with a lawyer to get the durable power of attorney and all that, which will be finished, but I was just curious. A lot of people try to do those type of things to avoid probate, and taxes, and Medicare risks, and all that, by transferring allotted assets into the children's name. I think that was about ten or 15 years ago before my mother passed and I think the rules have changed. Can you elaborate on that?

S1 59:55 And can you clarify the question just a little bit more.

S5 59:58 Sure. There used to be the ability to transfer all of the assets that an elderly person had into--

S1 60:07 To the children.

S5 60:08 --into the children's name. And I don't know if rules have changed to prevent that item so that they can get medicare assistance and all that kind of thing.

S1 60:20 We kind of talked about that a little bit yesterday, and we certainly--

S5 60:24 I didn't make it yesterday.

S1 60:24 -- we would address that today, so let's address it now. Good question. Thanks. [crosstalk].

S2 60:31 Carolyn just want to take that. I'll let Carolyn Rosenblatt take that.

S4 60:37 That's a complicated question and there is not a quick answer. But I will tell you several things to help you understand that. First of all, we're not taking about Medicare. Medicare is a federal program which ensures people over 65 or those who are totally disabled, they maybe younger, and they're able to get certain kinds of care paid for and it has nothing to do, at this point, with your income. Social Security and Medicare typically go together. When you're 65, right now it's changing, but when you're 65 right now you can qualify for Medicare. If you're talking about the state federal and county program of Medicaid, that's a completely different program. You must qualify for that by income. You're supposed to be poor. Whether you have intentionally impoverished yourself by giving away your property and your money, or you really don't have any money and you really are poor, you can qualify for Medicaid. If the idea of giving away your assets is to get you qualified for Medicaid so that you can live in a nursing home for the rest of your life and that's your intention, go right ahead. I don't recommend it. If someone has dementia and really has to be there and there's no other way to take care of them and the family doesn't have any alternatives, that's perfectly fine.

S4 61:52 But every state has some requirement in which they will look back - it's called the look-back provision - at how long ago the transactions of giving away property and money happened. And in most states I believe now it is five years. And also in all the states I've looked at, you can still keep your house and qualify for Medicaid if that is necessary for you to get Medicaid. But there are restrictions and reimbursement requirements in some states, and that's where the look-back provision comes in. It's kind of a complex subject. If that is an issue for you, I would strongly recommend that you get legal advice from an elder law attorney who specializes in Medicaid. The rules change all the time. They're going to change again, and with our county budgets and state budgets being so decimated now in this economy, I think there will be further action to restrict and limit intentional impoverishment in order to qualify for Medicaid.

S5 62:54 I understand. Thank you so much. My mother and father have passed so that did worked on in our favor for that. But for anybody else, I was just curious.

S1 63:03 That's a good question. Thank you, Vanessa. Thanks very much. I'm going to meet your line. Anyone else who has a question that who's listening on the line please press "star two" and you will go up to the top of the switchboard and I'll answer your question. If you're listening via webcast, you can write them in the box on the screen. Let me just check to see if new ones came in there because I have a whole bunch that came in before we started the broadcast. Ameenah and Carolyn B., I do want you to get involve in this. I know there's a lot of legal questions coming here but do jump in. Don't feel that it's all for Carolyn Rosenblatt. Question here from Judy in Wilson, Missouri. She's saying that her sister lives with her parents and is in-charge of their financial affairs. And the question is how can she, that is to say Judy, how can Judy gain legal access to her parents financial records to monitor questionable expenses?

S2 64:05 Is it the sister that's not living that wants to gain legal access to that?

S1 64:13 That's correct.

S2 64:14 I keep going back to the sibling contract. That's what she really needs to do because if she's on the outside looking in - excuse me for saying this - but why in the hell is she concerned if she's not doing any work? Why isn't she involved with that family? So, sibling contract, I believe, would be the way to go with that and that will cut down all--

S1 64:42 We can't judge. She may live 3,000 miles away or something, but the point is that she obviously has some concerns about the way the money's being spent, and people can exploit this. That was the thing. Is the sibling contract the only way to gain access to--

S2 65:02 We also have a mediator involved [crosstalk].

S4 65:07 I think that if she's an heir, a potential heir of the parents estate, then she has the right to know what's going on, and if possible that she could see an attorney and go to court and demand an accounting if her informal attempts to get an accounting of expenses have not been met. And this sometimes happens where there is something some hanky-panky going on, and the sibling from the outside looking in is suspicious. Sometimes the suspicions are unfounded. But in any case, the safest way if you're the caregiver sibling, is to be completely open and upfront, and keep good financial records, and share them with everybody else in the family so that you're not going to be falsely accused.

S2 65:46 Absolutely.

The Caregivers Legal Survival Guide

S1 65:50 Good morning. Did you have something to add to that?

S3 65:52 Yes. I wanted to say also with the new laws that I'm seeing even the one in Florida. They are specifying that good record keeping is part of the duty and the responsibility of the caregiver as well as the person who has the power of attorney. They need to be keeping good financial records so that they can have that available anyway. That should be something that her sibling should be keeping is good financial records anyway. But I know she wants to get access to that information. According to some of the laws, that sibling would have to have adequate record keeping, financial record keeping, and I don't know if that's happening in her state. But I know as the law has been enacted in Florida, I'm sure some of the other states are going to follow suit with making sure that these financial record keeping is looked at closely. So I think that's some of the things you're going to see change as time progresses on this issue. And it comes out that these loopholes are available for the financial abuse of both power of attorney and the financial and emotional abuse of caregivers as well as providers.

S3 67:20 And I want to make something clear. When I talk about caregiver or provider, I'm talking about a provider that may come in, that has been working as a paid person in a person's home as well, that provider and they abuse the rights of a senior. I know in one case where I was doing some work for an independent contracting work that I was doing, I encountered and actual abuse situation with an elder of a caregiver that was preferred provider and this gentlemen was trying to actually take her home by having her sign over her home to him. And she had told me that this is what was going on. So of course I felt I had a duty to report that, in which I did, and of course that incident was stopped, but we have many times that people or their providers that are being paid, they come in and financially abuse seniors. So this was going on quite often in California where people were taking elderly seniors homes. So this was a part of a trend of a part of a ring, I would say, band of people that were doing this and this was--

S1 68:47 Ameenah, if somebody's in that position, an elderly person, and they may be not have all of their physical strength or capacities, facilities-- faculties, that's the word I'm trying to find, faculties. Who do they call? Who do they contact when something like that might happen to them? What's their recourse?

S3 69:09 Well, that's why we have the Adult Protective Services. The elder abuse is supposed to be reported to Adult Protective Services and it's on that agency that they're supposed to investigate these issues of abuse. So they can call Adult Protective Services with legitimate claims of elder abuse, and also you can look at contacting, if it got really serious, you can also probably contact the district attorney's office as well. But I would say your first line of contact would be Adult Protective Services to report that type of elder abuse and immediately report it. And if you're someone that sees this type of abuse, I think it's on you to report it as well like I did. I reported it immediately because this lady literally begged me to help her and you cannot ignore that. Even though I wasn't her family member, I felt obligated to do my duty and report the abuse that I saw happening right before my eyes.

S4 70:22 And there is the 24-hour hotline for Adult Protective Services. A social worker will contact the elder. There's a public health nurse who sometimes will come out depending on the situation. They are very strapped and short staffed now because of budget cuts, once again, but their mandate across the US is to investigate reported or suspected elder abuse. And it does not have to be somebody trying to take their home. It can be a lot of different things. It's usually not the elder who calls and begs for help. It's somebody else--

S1 70:54 That's what I was saying. And so I was thinking that if my grandmother, back when she was deaf, blind and demented, if she had been in the care of somebody non-family person who was abusing her, I don't think she could have said anything. And also, my aunt who died in a nursing home in Brooklyn, I'm pretty sure that she was-- well, I won't go into it but I'm pretty sure that she had some real neglect. Not apart from the fact that she was dead for two days before they bothered to call my father. Actually, they didn't even call my father. He came to visit her and she was dead in the morgue for two days. And to me, that's abuse. I can't imagine that she could have called out for help. She didn't speak English, she was old--

S4 71:43 [inaudible] you can see why. The problem, just to give you an idea of the size of it, $2.6 billion per year is stolen from elders and money and property every year in the United States. And that number is rising.

S1 72:01 Well, it makes a bigger social issue which we're not going to get into tonight, but it really does have to do with bringing back a culture of loving our elders which is another huge issue that maybe we'll talk about another day. For now, I have a couple of other practical legal questions, and one is from Tiffany in [?] California. She's asking how many levels of conservatorship are there and which conservatorship forms should I be asking for?

S4 72:34 I don't think anybody can tell you should be asking for in a phone call with a stranger [but what I can say is that California [laughter] divides conservatorships into two parts. Conservatorship of the person, which has to do with your personal rights, your decision making, your ability to enter into contracts. All of that's taken away. And there's conservatorship of the estate which has to do with your money, your financial asset, your property. So you can have one or the other or you can have both. They can be limited or restricted by various agreements that are made ahead of time and submitted to the court, or the court will decide based on what the request, the petition looks like. But there is a lawyer who will petition for the conservatorship and there is a lawyer who will be appointed if they don't have one already for the person who is the proposed conservatee.

S1 73:29 Carolyn B., do you want to add something to say?

S2 73:32 I do want to just say one thing because this really brings everything to full circle as to my particular case. After I was dragged through three jurisdictions, I am basically having the restraining orders against me three different times. And I decided I wasn't going to try to fight it, I was too angry, too broken up, too physically exhausted. I started thinking I was going to have heart attacks the whole day. So I decided I'm not going to fight anymore because I had no more fight in me, and the last time we went before the judge, the same person that was looking for money, and this is kind of showing the difference between conservatorship of a person and also the financial conservatorship, this person and my family said, "Your honor, I've decided I only want medical. Give Carolyn the financial conservatorship." That's what she said after she discovered there wasn't any money. So that's why people really got to know what is really involved with taking care of a senior. Who's really paying for everything and if a family member, like myself, puts a whole binder together with all the medical records, all the financial records, look at it, look at the records. The records will actually show what's going on. So basically, the family member found out I was earning a really good income and that's why our father was able to stay in private assisted living the whole time I had him and trust me, it's not cheap. I was paying up to $6,500 a month for a tiny little room, a tiny little room for my dad to stay in. That did not include his medical, that did not include anything else, sure he was a veteran, but I just want people to know. Know what you're fighting for if you decide you want to be a caregiver, you don't know who's flipping those bills. And at the end, the sad part is that this person had to put our dad on welfare which really is very disturbing. So I just wanted to really show with conservatorship, there's two, there are the medical and also the financial.

S1 75:51 I think this might be the last-- sorry, Ameenah, did you have something to add to that too?

S3 75:56 Well, I wanted to say getting back to the power of attorney parts also with financial, with my grandmother's situation, that power of attorney also included the one that my aunt obtained. It included the mineral rights to oil that was part of my grandmother's estate. So it has implications financially, and this is what the problem is where you have a problem with what is that caregiver or what is the potential caregiver after, after a person loses their capacity? Are they after financial gain or are they really interested in taking care of that senior? So that is a question I think that needs to be answered in reference to the duty's of power of attorney and the financial obligations that a caregiver should already have in place. So they should have their finances in order that they're not attacking the seniors of state for their financial gain. And then I think it's important.

S1 77:17   Indeed. We've got one last question from Wanda in Alabama. She's just saying, "I want to know more about trust." Maybe we'll have a short tour of what's do we mean by trust. What are they? Why do we need them? When do we have them?

S4 77:35   Well, I think I should answer that probably because I'm the only lawyer here[laughter]. Let's just make this really basic and simple that anybody can get. A trust is basically like a box, a legal box. And you put things in it. And it has a certain status in the law. The trust is not a person. The trust is a thing. And that trust allows you to put stuff in it; property, goods, whatever that you own, money. And if you have that trust, you can have the people who are going to benefit from that trust get that stuff that's in the box when the person who creates the trust dies. And you don't have to go to court to do that. If you have a will, on the other hand, and what's in the will is not part of the trust- which is usually not a good way to do it- whatever is in the will that's supposed to go to the heirs, the beneficiaries, will have to be proven. Probate is what we try to avoid by having a trust. Probate is another way of saying proof or proving. That means you go to court. If all you have is a will, you're going to have to go to court and pay somebody to do that for you and it costs money. It's not free. It's expensive sometimes. Some laws allow the lawyer involved to take a percentage of what is in that will as a fee. So the best thing to do that most lawyers are going to tell you is put all your goods, your assets, your money into a trust including your home so that when that passes off to the heirs after you die, you do not have to go to court and pay somebody to administer that will. So that's kind of [inaudible] of what a trust is. Most lawyers are going to recommend that. I personally have my house in a trust for my kids and everything else I own is in a trust for my kids so that they're not going to have to deal with probate after I'm gone.

S1 79:29 Very interesting. Well, we have just a little while so I would like to just if Carolyn and Ameenah want to add to that, we'd just make it really short. So, go ahead and jump in and add to that, and then we have to kind of wrap it up.

S3 79:46 I want to add--

S2 79:47 Carolyn made it very, very simple. Very simple and thank you Carolyn for that explanation.

S4 79:53 You're welcome.

S3 79:55 I want to ask something--

S1 79:55 Ameenah?

S3 79:56 --I wanted to add one more item to that which is I know when my grandmother had a will and a trust, and the power of attorney or course existed while she was alive that my aunt obtained after she passed away which she passed away on Christmas day last year, that power of attorney also died with my grandmother. Now, my aunt tried to contain to use that power of attorney even though it died with my grandmother's death. And so the will had to come into play. The will had to be presented at the funeral home because my aunt interfered with that process even though my grandmother had all ready payed for those arrangements. She was trying to interfere with receiving medical record documentation and the will had to come forth. We actually had to pay a lawyer to actually go to court and let my aunt know that the power of attorney has died with the person and now the will was valid. So, sometimes it gets into that complication after someone has passed away that the will still has challenges to it. So, I know we experienced that and finally the will now has no more challenges because now the judge has put the order in and set forth that this will is valid. So, I think it's important for people to understand that, too, that a power of attorney dies when a person dies.

S1 81:37 That's a very good point.

S4 81:38 Yes, it's alive and it's dead when they're dead, and that just brings one last point which I want to make and that is if you're elder relative or you have put your estate planning documents together 20 or 30 years ago, please see somebody so that they can be updated. The laws changed. Maybe they weren't drafted very well. I have seen an awful lot of very poorly put together documents. So get them updated, get another look at it while the elder is still competent and capable of changing, or updating, or improving upon what they did in the first place.

S1 82:10 I just want to add one thing from a personal experience. Make sure that all the beneficiaries of the will or the trust understand what it says, because to me in a family situation, that's something that's something that caused an argument, because there was a difference in interpretation about what it meant, and that's something you want to avoid. So just make sure everybody understands it [chuckles] I think. Because it is complex. We have all these legal-- the legal jargon can be very complex, and people don't always understand what these documents say. I just want to let Carolyn B. do a little closing of what she'd like to just say as we're bring this to a close. And then I want to remind people of what's coming next. How you're going to get the audio for this, and about the book coming up, and stuff like that. Carolyn, how would you like to close this today?

S2 83:03 Well, the way I would like to close this is that first of all is just give honor to God for allowing me and selecting me to do this mission. I'm overwhelmed with joy to be able to have met the people along the journey that I've met. You included, Lynn, you're all the way in the United Kingdom. I mean, I would definitely want to come over and visit, and party, and-- it's just beautiful. And, Carolyn Rosenblatt that lives over and has a beautiful practice over in San Rafael, California, meeting Ameenah Fuller that's running for state senate, but on the same token, she's become a really good friend. So, I'm really honored. I pray that people would take this opportunity and take advantage of knowledge, because knowledge is truly powers. You don't have to say, "Well, I didn't know." I'm saying, "I didn't know." That's why I'm trying to help to empower every individual out there, if they care to have the knowledge. And thank all of my guests, all of my panelists, everyone, just thank you so much.

S1 84:10 And without any further ado, I want to thank our guests this evening, it was Ameenah Fuller, and Carolyn Rosenblatt. You will be receiving information on how to contact them and their websites in your email, maybe not tomorrow, maybe Monday. I'm still kind of pulling it all together. And you'll also receive the links to download all the audios on one page. Of course the audio to this conference will be available on this page within a couple of minutes of the conference ending. And do remember that Carolyn's book "Why Wait? the Baby Boomer's Guide to Preparing Emotionally, Financially, and Legally for a Parent's Death" is coming out on Tuesday, November 15th 2011. In case you happen to be listening to this three years from now [chuckles], I want to save the date. And do get the book. It will guide you through this process. Carolyn has consulted all of these guests who you've heard on the line or most of them in the process of researching this. And I think it'll give you a lot of comfort and also a lot of good information. And without any further ado, I'd like to wish you all a wonderful life and health and wealth and happiness and this is Lynn Serafinn from Spirit Authors. This has been the Why Wait? Telesummit. Good evening, good morning, and good night.

www.ingramcontent.com/pod-product-compliance
Lightning Source LLC
Chambersburg PA
CBHW070719210526
45170CB00021B/1078